I See Your Point You Moron!

A crucial 12-step program full of techniques for dealing with people whose opinions are different... and f*cking stupid

KAT and STEWART

Copyright © 2023 by Kat and Stewart
All rights reserved. This book or any portion thereof may not be reproduced or used in
any manner whatsoever without the express written permission of the publisher except
for the use of brief quotations in a book review.

Publishing Services provided by Paper Raven Books LLC

Printed in the United States of America

First Printing, 2023

Paperback ISBN: 979-8-9894978-2-9

Disclaimer:

Our attorneys, who we think are overly cautious but super cool, are making us tell you that these books are based on our personal histories and remedies that we discovered for ourselves and not psychological or medical advice for you, the reader.

I mean, we think we got this shit pretty well dialed in and we're crushing it right now, but hey… you do you. Legally.

Have you experienced any one of...

These scenarios?

THANKSGIVING.
Family table. Uncle MAGA is at one end, ranting about how the world has gone plumb-crazy, the Martians are coming, nobody is safe anymore, and some cult leader nobody has ever met or seen is the savior of us all. There's simply not enough wine in the world to deal with this.

WORK.
You're on a deadline and stressed, and you just need some help. Your new direct report, Wimpy McWoke-ster is all you have to rely on. He, she, or they are having a hard time dealing with your very reasonable requests. The pressure is a lot for them, and they weren't necessarily raised in a period where shared sacrifice was a thing. You're fucked and you figure you'll work faster on your own.

ONLINE.
You just wanted to post a nice little statement on world peace, your love of classic Michael Jackson or God (or Zeus) forbid a statement about equality. This naturally invites the most vicious responses, making you think you

must have accidentally added in "I love eating puppies for breakfast" or something. Your love for connection has given you an electronic black eye, and you wonder why you ever logged on at all.

HERE'S A WEIRD SECRET MOST PEOPLE WON'T TELL YOU OR AREN'T AWARE OF:

Everyone feels this way. Everyone is convinced they are right and if the world were more like them, everything would be perfect.

You too. Us too.

But that's impossible. We're all different and see the world differently from very unique perspectives.

But that doesn't mean that everyone has an opinion that deserves to be shoved down your throat. There are legitimately stupid fucking people out there, but they don't know it. They have no idea that they are the dummies.

In a town with a village idiot, everyone knows who the village idiot is except for one person: the village idiot.

Personally, we've both known our share of well-meaning morons who just can't seem to see reality right in front of them.

This book is a simple, 12-step communication program to help you navigate those lovable dummies and keep whatever sanity you have left.

Just like we did.

Be calm and understanding, follow the 12 steps of dealing with people whose stupid viewpoint deserves your best response, and know that sometimes, there's no response at all.

Step 1

UNDERSTAND THEY TRULY BELIEVE THEIR PERSPECTIVE IS VALID.

We've seen people say and do the stupidest things in the world, and they were absolutely convinced they were right.

But that doesn't take away the fact that they are dead wrong, and this is where empathy must take hold. Understand the stupid. Pity it. See if you can not let it affect you.

I See Your Point, **YOU MORON!**

Say this first part out loud:

- This moron is a few brain cells smarter than limestone.
- They probably think the same thing about me.
- Why do I have to deal with this fuck-tard?

Okay, good. You got that out of your system.

MANTRA FOR STEP 1:
THEY'RE NOT GOING AWAY.

Repeat after me:

- *I don't have to engage with them.*
- *I am responsible for my own responses.*
- *I have a lot of letting go to do.*

Great! That's the first step. When in doubt, if you're starting to feel like the person in front of you would have been better suited for a life in the circus, read Mantra for Step 1 again.

Step 2

CHANNELING YOUR INNER ZEN MASTER

Recognize that you are not responsible for teaching the dummies. They're dummies for a reason, they don't want to learn anything. If they did, they wouldn't be dummies. That's some deep Zen shit right there.

I See Your Point, YOU MORON!

Let's keep the real Zen shit going:

- Dummies don't want to change because they don't think they need to.
- They're not open to differing opinions.
- They prefer to be—and always think they are—right.
- I couldn't change them by teaching them more.
- How can I ask someone else to change, if I won't?

MANTRA FOR STEP 2:
AVOID THE URGE TO CHANGE MINDS

First, start with self-reflection. Look in the mirror and ask yourself "Could it be me?" If you're asking, then the answer is no.

Repeat after me:

- *I was convinced that arguing with a dummy would teach them something new and they would see my point.*
- *I am responsible for my own growth, not theirs.*
- *But I think I'm understanding what my path should look like instead of building up frustration over something I'm unable to control.*
- *Damn…I have a shit ton of work to do!*

Step 3

BE A LISTENER, NOT A DEBATER.

Rather than engaging in heated debates, lend an ear to understand their viewpoints. It's like taking an anthropological journey!

I See Your Point, **YOU MORON!**

Time for a real shift in thinking:

- If you're trying to prove you're right, you're spending time talking, not listening.
- You might have set up your life where you were always the correct one.
- Take an honest look—phone a friend.

MANTRA FOR STEP 3:
JUST MAKING SURE IT'S NOT ME.
Let's try this…

Repeat after me:

- *My need to be right may sometimes jeopardize my friendships.*
- *I should talk with a friend that I trust to see if I might be the moron here. Am I actually a good listener?*
- *Feedback is crucial. Seek it out and don't be afraid of the answers.*
- *Remember, you're just making sure. People are still dummies. You just want to be more self-aware.*

Step 4

ENHANCE YOUR LISTENING SKILLS TO INCLUDE 'SELECTIVE HEARING'.

Learn the art of hearing only the important parts of their arguments and ignore the rest. Let the "stupid" fade away.

Time for a little real real:

- The more passion, the more the need to express it.
- Listen, if you can, for what they're really saying.
- What does the dummy in your life need to get out?

MANTRA FOR STEP 4:
WE'RE ALL HUMAN AFTER ALL.

Action items:

- Make a list of the people who drive you batshit crazy—or who are batshit crazy.
- Ask yourself: "How did they get this way?"
- See if you can listen for the meaning behind the meaning.
- Example: "The World Is Flat!"

Okay, so, no… but what was it that led you to this conclusion? Why do you need to believe this?

Step 5

AVOID THE URGE TO CHANGE THEIR MIND.

Release the superhero urge to convert everyone to your way of thinking. Let each person have their own "special" opinions.

Let Go!

This is the hardest thing to do, until you realize that you are doing the very same thing they are doing—forcing opinions.

Nobody needs to be right, and yet we work so hard at it! Why?

Ask yourself if you know.

Possible answer: *Because I am right!*

Yeah, that makes sense, and it's probably true. Unless you think that Zolton dropped us off here from planet Taint and we're all here to serve the mighty overlord.

MANTRA FOR STEP 5:
LET THEM BE WRONG!

Here's why: How many times have you changed your opinion when someone told you that you were stupid for having it? Not many, I would guess. (Unless it was Kat, she really is always right!)

Action Item:

Practice making a space for the idiot in your life to be an idiot. And don't worry, in the next few steps we're going to be working on the subtle art of friendly persuasion.

Step 6

CHANNEL YOUR INNER SOCRATES.

It can't hurt to understand the mind of the dumbass in front of you. Get curious. Start by asking thought-provoking questions. Make them ponder their own viewpoints while scratching their heads.

I See Your Point, **YOU MORON!**

This is an art form, that if mastered, can change minds and be entertaining!

When the dummy says something dumb, allow them to complete what they're saying and ask clarifying questions—as if you were interested in learning more. You might be surprised by what you hear!

- Wait, really? The Earth is flat? How do you know? Who told you?
- Aliens live among us? Wow! Have you met one?
- Your political rival is the manifestation of Satan? What is it about that person that actually screams Spawn of Evil?

MANTRA FOR STEP 6:
STAY COOL, INVESTIGATE.

Here's an example: (and this actually happened with Stewart)

Dummy: "I know for a fact that the Earth is flat and we're living under a dome."
You: "Wow, that's cool. How do you know for sure?"
Dummy: "Because oxygen and other gasses in the atmosphere can't be held down, they must escape. How could they stay near the Earth's surface without being contained under a dome? It's scientifically impossible."
You: "Oh wow, interesting point. Let me ask you…

air is made of molecules, right? And molecules have mass, right?"

Dummy: "Uh, yeah…"

You: "So, because we're all held to the surface by gravity, and molecules have mass, which gravity attracts, wouldn't air—which actually has mass—be held down by gravity too?"

Dummy:

You: "I mean, the air is thicker at the surface and thinner the higher you go up. If we were under a dome, the air would be the same thickness from top to bottom, right?"

Dummy:

At some point you'll have a chance to get them thinking, just by the question you ask.

Step 7

PLAY DEVIL'S ADVOCATE

Flip the script and argue passionately for their "stupid" opinion. By doing so, you'll expose the flaws and contradictions within their own argument.

I See Your Point, **YOU MORON!**

This is truly an art form and one that really just serves to tickle your own funny bone. But what the hell, life is short. Here are some basics:

Let them have their say. Listen intently. Let them finish.
Then repeat back to them exactly what they said with interest.
Remember, they need to believe this! It doesn't matter why. So, adopt the 'Curiosity Stance', approached their perspective as if studying a fascinating, yet perplexing new species.
"So, you're saying that lizard people are living amongst us right now…? Have you met any? Do they shed every summer? Can I meet one?'"

MANTRA FOR STEP 7:
TOY WITH THEIR DELUSIONS.

Remember, you're still being respectful.

Action items:

- Play along.
- Get good at being fascinated—you'll never get them to see your point of view anyway.
- Have some fun making them say the stupid part out loud.

Step 8

LEARN TO WALK AWAY.

Sure, being right is important, and yes, you're right about certain things.

And yes, it's super annoying when a moron has a soap box and an ounce of legitimacy.

But you're smarter. And smart means mature.

I See Your Point, YOU MORON!

Remember yourself:

Find joy in the knowledge that you're not a moron, a dummy, a rube.

Laugh at how silly you are when you actually get upset with stupid people. If you're pissed off, they're winning!

It's been said that the more intelligent a person is, the more they are miserable. We agree. But that's only because we spend so much time railing against the dummies!

MANTRA FOR STEP 8:
LIVE AND LET LIVE—WITH DISTANCE!

Action items:

- Realize what you've learned so far—you can't change them, pass the salt
- "Why should I change, they're the dumb one!?" doesn't get you anywhere. They have no desire or ability to change. But you do. And your misery quotient lowers when you learn to let people be who they are.
- Set up boundaries. Use the techniques described in this book to separate yourself from the moron in your life.

Step 9

FIND YOUR PEOPLE, BUT BE WARY OF TRIBES.

Surround yourself with like-minded friends and family who operate at your level. There are just as many of you as there are of them. Find your tribe and connect!

I See Your Point, **YOU MORON!**

What makes us miserable:

We're most miserable when we can't get the moron to understand our point or feel like we have to force our perspectives onto them.

Either way, we lose and that's a recipe for misery.

You know it because you wouldn't be reading this book if you didn't experience this exact frustration. That, or you just liked the title and you're enjoying this on the commode.

MANTRA FOR STEP 9:
THE WORLD IS BIG ENOUGH FOR US ALL!

Congregate with your people but learn to understand the moron. Understanding goes a long way towards acceptance and peace.

And that's ultimately what you want.

ACTION ITEMS:

- Catch yourself when you judge and pigeonhole someone.
- See if the reason is more than just being annoyed by them.
- Ask yourself seriously… is there any redeeming quality I could find in them?
Hint: There is.

Step 10

BASED ON YOUR UNDERSTANDING, ATTEMPT TO FIND COMMON GROUND.

Wars are based on differences we chose to not overcome because we couldn't start with mutual understanding or respect.

I See Your Point, YOU MORON!

No one wakes up planning to ruin another person's day. Comradery is an intentional choice, but so are anger and division.

You have the ability to choose anything you want each day. What are you choosing?

MANTRA FOR STEP 10: **ACCEPT AND ALLOW!**

You have it within you to influence others. You're smart and interesting. Often, the moron in your life continues to be so because they didn't have anyone to invest in them.

The more we ignore or shame the dummy, the more they will fill the resultant gap with their own stupid thoughts. You can be the change they need to see!

ACTION ITEMS:

- Listen, accept, and acknowledge.
- Invest in their existence. Let them know you hear them.
- Create trust between you so they will begin to listen to you.

The No.1 reason an idiot is an idiot is because they needed someone to accept them. There are forces out there preying on that need and filling the dummy's mind with poison to win them over.

Seriously… you could help. If you wanted.

Now, if the dummy doubles down after all this and wants to enroll you in a ride on the next Space Bus coming to take us to Venus, well then, all bets are off.

As Albert Einstein once wrote: "Two things are infinite: the universe and human stupidity; and I'm not sure about the universe."

Step 11

LEARN TO TRULY UNDERSTAND THE IDIOT.

The King, Elvis, sang "Walk a Mile In My Shoes." Granted, his shoes at that point were four-inch, blue suede platforms that could support Andre the Giant, but hey, the point is still valid. Let's explore it.

I See Your Point, YOU MORON!

The dummy chooses not to grow. Make no mistake about it, that's a choice.

But there's a reason behind it. And nearly every time that reason can be fear.

MANTRA FOR STEP 11:
I HAVE COMPASSION FOR YOU.

There's a great saying; "Never judge anyone for their behavior, you have no idea what they're going through."

We've talked about strategies to not encourage or shame the fool before us. But now it's time to use the tool that sets us apart: empathy.

Action items:

- Take a journey into their minds
- If you have to, invent a past that explains their behavior
- If you're familiar with their past, then that's easier for you

There's a saying; "In life we get hit by a truck early on. As a result, some of us become the truck, others stay the victim, and even fewer of us become the ambulance.

We all get struck. So, which one are you?

The ambulance folks (and the victims to an extent) have a keen understanding of the pain of the truck hitting us. The truck does not. That sucks. But it doesn't take away from the fact that the truck was once not the truck. This is where empathy must take the place of judgment.

Step 12

CHOOSE YOUR FRIENDS AND LEAVE THE REST—AND YOURSELF—IN PEACE.

This is the secret sauce. The letting go with love. The boundaries, the guardrails, the safety nets. All of it. This is your key to sanity.

I See Your Point, YOU MORON!

Part of the trap of having empathy is that often the dummy counts on that to garner attention, whatever form that takes.

MANTRA FOR STEP 12: CHOOSE WISELY AND SET BOUNDARIES

Does this person fit into my way of life, my thinking, my beliefs? They don't have to. And just because you had a relationship with them before doesn't mean you have to continue it. Even with family members!

But this is entirely up to you to decide… are they in or out?

Action items:

- Make a list of the people in your life
- Create two columns: "Things I can tolerate" | "Things I can't tolerate"
- Choose the first person and fill in the columns.

Here's a hint; if you're choosing a person, that likely means you've already decided they are on the bubble in the first place

If it's a spouse or partner, check out I Forgive You, You Psycho! (shameless plug!). One of the pieces of wisdom we share in that book is: "When someone shows you who they are—believe it."

If someone is lucky enough to have fewer mentions in

the "Things I can't tolerate" column, then it's up to you to learn to set boundaries. Remember why you're friends in the first place and refocus your attention on those aspects of that person.

Best of luck out there!

Notes

"TYPES" OF MORONS:

1. **The Eternal Know-It-All**: This person always has an answer, even when it's blindingly wrong. They're the human version of "Stupid Google without filters."

2. **The Contrarian**: No matter what you say, they'll take the opposite stance just for the thrill of disagreement. It's their own personal sport. They revel in their own confidence.

3. **The Conspiracy Theorist**: Brace yourself for a whirlwind of unusual explanations and secret society revelations. Remember, the truth is out there (maybe). This moron is especially dangerous because it votes.

4. **The One-Upper**: Prepare for a never-ending battle of who has the better story, accomplishment, or life experience. They always top it, no matter what you share.

5. **The Perpetual Pessimist**: Everything is doom and gloom with this person. Their glass is not only half empty, but it's also leaking. They live to poison the moment with their own dour attention-grabbing bullshit.

6. **The Endless Rambler**: Settle in, because this person never stops talking. Buckle up for a never-ending monologue. You wait and wait for them to take a breath, but they seem to not need one. And every word is just painfully stupid.

7. **The Dramatist**: They're upset about everything! Everyone is wrong, no one gets it—everyone is STUPID! And if you ever make any sense to them, they fall into a puddle of tears as you've just penetrated their worldview—and hurt their feelings.

8. **That one Uncle**. 'Nuff said.

www.ingramcontent.com/pod-product-compliance
Lightning Source LLC
Chambersburg PA
CBHW051617010526
44119CB00008B/188